FUTURE WORKS

ALSO BY **JEFF DERKSEN**

After Euphoria
Annihilated Time: Poetry and Other Politics*
Down Time*
Dwell*
Memory Is the Only Thing Holding Me Back
Transnational Muscle Cars*
Until

AS EDITOR
Scree: The Collected Earlier Poems, 1962–1991 by Fred Wah*

AS A MEMBER OF URBAN SUBJECTS
Autogestion, or Henri Lefebvre in New Belgrade
The Militant Image Reader
Momentarily: Learning from Mega-events
The Possibilities Are

* Published by Talonbooks

FUTURE WORKS

POEMS

JEFF DERKSEN

TALONBOOKS

© 2025 Jeff Derksen

All rights reserved. No part of this book may be reproduced, stored in a retrieval system, or transmitted, in any form or by any means, including machine learning and AI systems, without the prior written consent of the publisher or a licence from Access Copyright (the Canadian Copyright Licensing Agency). For a copyright licence, visit accesscopyright.ca or call toll-free 1-800-893-5777.

Talonbooks
9259 Shaughnessy Street, Vancouver, British Columbia, Canada V6P 6R4
talonbooks.com

Talonbooks is located on xʷməθkʷəy̓əm, Sḵwx̱wú7mesh, and səlilwətaɬ Lands.

First printing: 2025

Typeset in Guyot
Printed and bound in Canada on 100% post-consumer recycled paper

Cover: *Terminal V*, 1969, by Pierre Coupey
Inside front cover: *Urban tree Cairo* by Jeff Derksen
Inside back cover: *Urban tree Vienna* by Sabine Bitter

Talonbooks acknowledges the financial support of the Canada Council for the Arts, the Government of Canada through the Canada Book Fund, and the Province of British Columbia through the British Columbia Arts Council and the Book Publishing Tax Credit.

Library and Archives Canada Cataloguing in Publication

Title: Future works : poems / Jeff Derksen.
Names: Derksen, Jeff, 1958- author.
Identifiers: Canadiana 20240479327 | ISBN 9781772016284 (softcover)
Subjects: LCGFT: Poetry.
Classification: LCC PS8557.E5895 F88 2025 | DDC C811/.54—dc23

To Roy Miki,

for changing the language

I think of a tree

to make it

last.

LORINE NIEDECKER

New Goose

TABLE OF CONTENTS

1	More than Human Labour
7	Forty Days and Eight Hundred Nights
11	In Memory of My Heavy Metal Years
16	Living Through Aluminum
26	More Poems about Books and Records
31	All Day Long and into the Night
35	I Approve the Minutes
39	How to Keep Breathing in the Future
43	Time to Get It Together
45	My Short Novel
47	My Hard Edge Paintings
48	Conceptualism After Minimalism
50	Time Catches
62	Late Fascism, Early Afternoon
63	A Sad Gain
66	The Most Beautiful Thing

URBAN TREES

68	are all trees urban now?
69	willow trees for lost lagoon
70	address to the city
71	a city's idea of itself (political economy of trees)
72	address to a country tree
73	trees and shelter
74	"the battle over Sheffield's street trees"
75	future trees
76	workers' cuffs
77	brownfield pussy willows
78	bombing soil
79	bombing trees
80	neurological canopy
81	ungovernable trees
82	trees in "The Indian Act, 1876"
83	"Should Trees Have Standing?"
84	searching for the comrade tree
85	tree cities of the world

89	Notes on Sources, References, and Inspirations
93	Acknowledgments
95	Thank You

MORE THAN HUMAN LABOUR

for Hvaldimir

Obsolete cold-war navy dolphins write algorithms that design an app to do the laundry for overemployed people.

Dung beetles, decommissioned from nature documentaries, collectively lug overweight luggage into the cargo bays of discount European airlines.

The bats who took a short-term contract to patrol a new condo construction site at night to thwart theft from "the midnight lumberyard" are injured when the beam they hang on to take their break collapses.

Metallica replaces their drummer with an octopus from Vigo, Spain, who learned heavy metal on the sides of the ships they once riveted on the waterfront.

Acrobatic barn swallows dust the penthouses of oligarchs, poetically catching each mote in the air.

Turf wars break out between European and Chinese praying mantids; the deadly squabbles end through negotiations by unemployed European parliamentarians who lost their jobs when elected political positions were opened to all species.

Whales tow tankers through the rushing tidal waters into Vancouver's harbour, having joined the Canadian Merchant Service Guild.

Uniformed skunks, working in groups, keep protesters away from the pipeline, raising their tails and spraying directly into the eyes of civil citizens in accord with their training ordinances.

Horses block the street for the filming of a scene in a movie in which a detective team of a crow and a raven try to solve the case of a missing city politician (themself a barred owl who migrated to the city), racking up double-time wages for the work.

The goats who do the landscaping for the city have gone on strike, asking for fewer working hours and more variety in their food; the city responded by bussing in a road gang of llamas from a local prison.

Are the krill done with the dishes yet?

Have those little non-union fish completed the pedicure?

Do rufous hummingbirds sleep on the job?

Has the sloth put the baby to sleep?

Have the trout completed their microcredentials?

Have the Steller's jays negotiated a new contract yet?

Banana slugs wearily lead tourists through the park's marshland area, having texted the red-winged blackbirds when they should flash up, display their underwings, and sing.

Raccoon sous-chefs prepare another locally sourced meal at restaurants bearing such names as Forage, Terrain, West, Sea, Park.

Organized pollens clog voting machines in Iowa.

The woodpeckers who carve seamless single-tree replicas of Danish modern furniture from live teak planted in the formerly deforested Amazon are challenged in court by the copyright holders of Arne Jacobsen's iconic Ant chair.

Weaver birds silently stitch wounds in the emergency wards of privatized hospitals – and fly home to elaborate nests, catching some sleep before their next shift.

During their northward migrations, grey whales hold workshops up and down the coast on horizontalism and radical democracy.

Software-writing squirrels in Latvia keep one step ahead of the cyberpolice, working in intensive bursts, stepping aside as a comrade takes their spot in the code chain.

Kermode bears plot anarchy high in the mountains but find urban warfare difficult.

Bluefin tuna, running in schools at high speed, overtake luxury yachts, force the owners into rescue dinghies, and redistribute the loot through complex supply chains of defunct sushi markets.

A tourist buys a bracelet from a starfish on the beach in Rovinj, Croatia; the starfish dreams of the olden days of Yugoslavia, of social wealth.

Bavarian boars, pushed into cities by new land enclosures, work with tent villages in urban parks, fending off city crews given orders to tear down the camps. Students organize protests in solidarity with the boars.

Slovakian bears, trained on early electronic keyboards and synthesizers, begin a successful electronic music record label in Vienna.

Ants close down the North American banking system with a highly coordinated strike on ATMs: over New Year's Eve, individual bills are carried out of the machines, moved along predetermined routes, and stashed in complex underground networks. Two ants are captured but refuse to give up their comrades. In solidarity, they eat each other.

Diplomatic pandas negotiate new trade restrictions on the production of electric cars.

Twelve sheep from Salt Spring Island establish a craft brewery in East Vancouver; a group of Norwegian grey rats chew through the gentrifier's distillery hoses and reclaim the neighbourhood.

Mice and guinea pigs care for the elderly in Maple Ridge.

Blue algae shut down the tourist industry in Washington State and set up an unseen alternative society.

Robins grade the multiple-choice final exams of first-year university students after students complain that the mallard ducks who did it last year, brought in on contract, were too erratic and had nervously shit on the test booklets.

A forty-year-old halibut wins a seat for the Green Party in Tofino, BC.

A black squirrel wins the 24 Hours of Le Mans race but is tragically killed crossing the track after victory.

Vietnamese pot-bellied pigs from San Francisco again win the International Street Food Epicurean award for their Asian-fusion vegetarian cuisine.

Vast multitudes of freshwater mussels decolonize rivers by incrementally covering obsolete hydroelectric dams.

Razor clams lie undetected under the sand of Malibu, burrowing closer to beach mansions.

Peregrine falcons, in high-speed graceful descents, deliver Swiss watches to each participant of the Davos World Economic Forum before elegant geese serve foie gras to the titans of commerce.

Costa Rican parrots, working for a third-party outsourcer, make robocalls for political parties, fanning misinformation and fake voting locations across the USA and Canada.

Great blue herons open a successful sushi bar – called Great Blue Heron – and are featured in *Dwell* magazine (which is edited by a group of Oxford-trained Welsh corgis).

Mycelium protest their representation in the media and demand control over their own image.

The crow who designed early HTML is found living in a commune outside of Berlin, composing collectively played ambient music and designing social-media software planned for free global downloading.

New mosquito variants relay information regarding viruses back to national health organizations.

In the civic aquariums they methodically occupied, sea anemones lead slow-living workshops for humans.

Sand dollars are devalued.

Long-distance-truck-driving barn owls congregate at a 24-hour diner in Golden, BC.

Manta rays take out the underwater internet cables and are counterattacked by schools of CIA mackerel.

A flock of pigeons, gone wildcat after being fired from Amazon as delivery apparatuses, down a police drone as it hovers unseen above their shipping warehouse.

The Office of Wasp Architects (OWA) wins the Pritzker Architecture Prize for their social-housing project, constructed from chewed wood and pinesap, that covers the slopes of West Vancouver.

A group of self-schooled pigs clone human organs in a decommissioned tractor factory in Upper Austria.

Starlings in the park act spontaneously – against the wishes of the orderly geese hierarchy.

Tapeworms provide individual biofeedback on "gut health" in exchange for housing.

Dust mites relay your sleeping data back to memory-foam mattress makers.

After successfully suing for name copyright infringement, kangaroos establish urban food-delivery networks for "the creative class."

Phosphorescent cookiecutter sharks guide the way for human migrants in boats, those forsaken by other humans, while pilot whales form a boundary against Italian naval authorities.

A long lineup at the Vintage Bazaar for quick tattoos by a red-necked avocet, a self-taught artist specializing in small-insect tattoos.

Songbirds provide the final day of care in palliative wards.

Sturgeons patiently wait for the "historically ripe moment."

FORTY DAYS AND EIGHT HUNDRED NIGHTS

I felt, but I could not tell – I did not know.

We fell – into an order.

The city too amended its pace.

The streets responded in kind, in time.

I mistook the seconds for imperatives and the clock became the park behind our apartment.

The day became a department.

Work became time, dispersed through every space.

We looked out over the port as it took a slow rhythm.

"Forty days and forty nights, like a ship out on the sea."

The economy appeared as movements – imagined as chains.

As a measure and a condition – chain or chains.

The economy needed to keep moving between and through cities and people.

The economy needed to be saved above all.

Lower labour became essential and care was work.

Is it you and the economy or the economy and me?

"We are all in this together" and some are more in than others.

"We are all in this together" and some will get more out of it than others.

There was a brief moment when it was clear money could simply be printed.

It was ink.

That we had invented it, and we could make it.

Its mystique had quietly folded, it was no longer a bond binding.

Even rent stopped its expansion – it did not need to exist.

From the highest heights to the deepest debt.

When it returned, it returned as a *visible divinity*.

Nature was *not* in it.

We were bending away from breath like a possible moment of death.

We had taken distancing measures.

Contact tracing made us bodies of information.

In the origin of blame, a woman wearing a mask on Denman Street was slapped in the face.

There were variants of concern.

We needed to concede surveillance.

Or concede for the health of others.

Then the police were inside everywhere, a spectacular form.

Inside was eternal, a permeated convention.

Households were bubbles in a reduction.

Work at home standing on top of your hours, your own hours.

Domestic slipped into *work*, so now time is a line from screen to bed.

People could unravel and not be seen.

And then the birds returned.

And other things that needed air or silence.

The noise in the sea was a different listening.

An opposite rhythm of recession and expansion.

The rhythm of the broken chain opened spaces.

Into those spaces things fell.

The stability of things fell.

Food fell into spaces that were once felt to be seamless.

The space of food could not be overcome.

The labour of California moved our food.

The flood that broke the chain of the food.

The lake that was always a lake came back.

The fires that slowed supply.

The fires that cut roads.

The border that was reordered for block and flow.

Imagined regions were borders through the thick political space.

Covering the surface of the earth, broken logistics without a logic.

It was still invisible, but you could *feel* it.

Students who were bodies were to feel it.

With the restart lifting began.

I was Step Four of the restart.

By what were we all connected?

Then connections frayed.

IN MEMORY OF MY HEAVY METAL YEARS

There goes the aluminum
the antimony, the arsenic, the barium
the cadmium, the cesium, the gadolinium
the lead, the mercury, the nickel
the thallium, and the tin.

There goes that job spraying lawns
with chemicals, driving the Merc
three-quarter ton
with a tank on the back
and no brakes
through West Vancouver, bouncing
the wheels against the curb
to stop
on the steep magisterial streets
that afford such views

that they could hire
two talentless dickbrains
to weed and feed
front and back
and back again
in two weeks.

That was a heavy metal job
that probably killed
a lot of salmon too.

There goes the shotgun
pellets from the pheasants
we shot out in Abbotsford and Langley
plucked and hung
in the concrete basement

in New Westminster
fresh with the stink
of pheasant guts.

There goes that summer painting
the house with my brother
wire-brushing off
the old paint, breathing
it in on the wooden ladders

white guys working
on a tan
and saving up
for the Peugeot ten-speed.

There goes the seventies
out from my body.
Led Zep Humble Pie Burning Spear, and
Marley too, adidas, big E Levi's
from Kelly's Men's and Boy's Wear on Sixth Ave.
there goes that brown shingle house
paint, broken down
and pissed out.

There goes those years
beachcombing along the Fraser
from New West to Lulu Island
pulling out cedar blocks
that had floated free
from the shake-factory booms.

Pulling the blocks out
of that industrial muck

grey-green and foamy
down near Scott Paper, the mill

that Larry worked in until
it moved production south.

Then stacking and drying the blocks
to split them into shakes
with a birchwood
hammer and an adze.

There goes that industrial mix
from the Fraser
from the riverbank
from the bars by the river.

There goes sucking on
a hose to get some gas into that
golden sixty-six Valiant convertible
with the leaky roof and
the 273 and putting it
right into the carb to sputter
the piece of shit to life
again. Still, pretty great

to have a convertible with a radio
(turn the radio on
roadrunner roadrunner!)
and a five-gallon gas can
and a piece of garden hose

and a mouthful of
Regular, a mouthful of
Regular Leaded
from the Chevron
in the strip mall across Tenth Ave.

There goes working
on a printing press

under the sidewalk
of the storefront at Cambie and Hastings
that was later the Caribbean place.

There goes that time.

There goes all the shitty renos
on West Broadway, on Hastings, on Commercial Drive,
there goes the dust
from that wall Mike took down
with a chainsaw
when Talonbooks was above the foundry
and there goes the foundry dust
and the sweep of chemicals
that would take your head off
like six beers later at the Waldorf.

There goes the mystery
unmarked jars of cleaners
and solvents and grease
that Larry nicked from the mill
and we used on the cars and bikes
and on our hands.

There goes that job at the self-serve
Shell with a car wash across from the college
when it was in temporary trailers
just to show that education
for the masses
was taken seriously.

And there goes the dust
and everything from that week
in September
when what was stored in the three
buildings of the World

Trade Center was pulverized
and burned into the air
and Nancy and I stayed in the apartment
with T-shirts tied
over our mouths and noses

and didn't go out until
we went to Milano's
where the firefighters drank for free
with the IRA guys
leaning at the bar.

There goes the
aluminum, the antimony, the arsenic
the barium, the cadmium
the cesium, the gadolinium
the lead, the mercury
the nickel, the thallium, and
the tin. Broken down
pissed out.

There goes those jobs, those times
there goes those relations
of inside and outside, of work
and nerves and fat and soft tissue
and synapses.
There goes that set of relations
inside and outside.

There goes that body
that use and surplus.

LIVING THROUGH ALUMINUM

after Pat Lowther

In my mind
I am walking back
through a country
or a town
that no longer exists
with my father
who lost his job
to robots

who ran the machines
he worked on.

He never *lost*
his job to a robot
invasion. There was
never an inversion
of the future
without humans –
in the end
it was lung cancer
from breathing paper.

We had a father-son project
that did not involve
drunkenness and cruelty
but just some coal
that we were compressing
first by hand
then by pressure
a long-term bonding
project with a goal

to sell the coal
once it was diamond
in order to retire.

Then the price
of coal skyrocketed
because of China
or a boom that followed a bust
and we could not afford
the raw material.

Our growing target market
only wanted better diamonds
rockets, rent, cowboy hats
and everything.

We pushed the car instead:
it had been sitting
battery dead.

"As the dead prey upon us
they are dead in themselves"
I had misread
and that misreading

led me to dread
the forms of total emptiness
on offer.

But today I realize
everything I am feeling
fear glee euphoria utility
is grandly shaped
by what others
perhaps dead
will say or do

or invade bomb kneel on
crash burn and dispossess.

Sadly, today I spin in
the whirling superstructures
in the sky
and on the earth –
moments and decisions
of humans whether
it is May or September.

Such an autumnal May
can spark decision fatigue
or flames that rip
through towns villages
territories in a new season
called *fire*.

This fatigue or these flames
affect my performance
in the workplace
where I perform labour
and also feel it.

A president might say
or do something
as they whirl above
and that affects the lives
of millions and they
might notice that.

Is that labour?
Who is fit
for the job? Whose mind
and heart can
pump long enough?

What can democracy
demonstrate – a paradox
for young and old
or data-driven decisions:
a majority of people
disagreed
with the war criminal.

"No more war crimes" could
have been the ignored call
across most of my life:
resistance persistence and then
another long wave.

We know where
Kissinger is now
a legacy of a *statesman*
who made "the economy
scream"
to the end of time.

It could scream
hallelujah now. Hey
Leonard Cohen make Henry Kissinger
scream, make him sing
"Te Recuerdo Amanda"
until the end of time
which will not end
and the wet street
with the factory.

The better ending
would be the economy
screaming back
back from Chile
No pasarán, or *basta*

this economy is ours
no surplus

or loudly to today
"no more war crimes!"

"no more Pinochets"

which should
not need to be
a universal cry.

No cancer, no coal
no diamonds
and no Pinochet
in our future or
even in our past

even though it's the present
I'm worried about
when it comes
to the future.

What would the earth
the rocks the trees
all say to this: Is
that fair to ask?

Or, not their job?

It's a forever chemical
if it is in you
forever. That's why
I can't abide the aluminum
I'm writing on

another neurotoxin
blocking synapses
just when I want
to work them.

Aluminum and bauxite owe
a big apology to Haiti
historically and in the present.

So do those hydroelectric
turbines and I guess the guys
who engineered the dam
and the workers who built
the Kenney Dam.

And those who only
gave (*gave*) the Cheslatta
Carrier four days to pack up
before the land, the villages
were flooded under.

A normal natural disaster
that capitalism makes
and needs
for energy.

The whirl of northern turbines
with southern bauxite
screaming.

The dam hums out
"surplus electricity"
that is sold to power
the grid, the power grid
when the bauxite
is not cooking, somewhere

or so I imagine in my mind
a product of those same
churnings, of that same
power.

The lights of Los Angeles
are beautiful against
the dark. You know that
shot from movies, the grid
of streets seen from the hill
through a modernist window.

The water is made to work
to churn bauxite
to alumina, caustic soda
and lime, then
carbon and electricity.

The villages and Ancestors
are still under
that working water.

Why do I think Alcan
had bauxite mines
in Haiti throughout my life?

How has that defined my life
even though
I have never been to Haiti
or known the first revolution.

But Sean Penn, starring
as Sean Penn white saviour
drops in heroically, helicopters
to the island of the original
revolution to lend some muscle
and extract some footage.

Now Guinea is where
bauxite resources "overlap"
with "Indigneous and/or
peasant land"
for future aluminum.

My computer cannot apologize
as if it were a trained official
to Haiti or to the Cheslatta
or to Guinea
and/or to me
for it is an object
made assembled designed
across places, conditions
we can't know about

that's a classic – hide it
all with a seamless
surface, boxed fresh
shipped as if from air
as if with no past
and a disassembled
future.

Pinochet had dropped dreaming
socialists into the ocean
from helicopters made
with aircraft-grade aluminum.

One of these helicopters
found new work
in a park where people
play combat. Another use.

How to say all of this.

Later this computer
when it is no longer
working, has no work
could be barged over the ocean
a waste export
stripped and boiled of its useable
metals by boys in the scrap economy
without protection.

Then this computer
an unthinking product

of a modern smelter
and other facts and acts
and labour
with tailings and emissions.

"With the older smelter,
there was lots of problems, lots
of sickness. And now,
with the modern smelter,
hopefully, we get rid of all
those problems that
we can have better air quality."

and that's a wave
of progress

and who doesn't want better air
or progress
even those in another world
or under water or dirt.

If there is too much to know
about aluminum, labour
Haiti, Chile, Kissinger

about Agbogbloshie, the Chelsatta
and Guinea and Sean Penn
and Puma helicopters
and/or overlap

how do we know it
to compress it
to continue breathing
in the future

MORE POEMS ABOUT BOOKS AND RECORDS

Dear Diane, I have your Cat Stevens's *Teaser and the Firecat*, with "Diane" written in ink above that last *S* in his name.

Dear Sid Zlotnik, the receipt for the copy of K. Marx, *Capital*, vol. 1, that you bought for $1.56 on October 4, 1954, at People's Co-operative Bookstore at 337 W. Pender St. is still tucked inside the front cover.

Dear Elaine, you wrote your name over Al Green's hand on the cover of *Let's Stay Together*, which I now have (original Hi Records copy!) – why did you part with it, did it not mend your broken heart?

Dear K.D., I still have your copy of Louis Althusser's *Lenin and Philosophy* you gave me when you left Vancouver the first time: its spine is cleanly broken at page 114.

McDonald, you printed your name neatly on the upper-left corner of the back cover of Billy Joe Royal's *Down in the Boondocks* that I picked up yesterday.

Dear Laurie Hunter, I have your copy of Eldridge Cleaver's *Soul on Ice* that you likely got as it was taken out of circulation from Vancouver Public Library's Collingwood Branch.

Dear Doreen, I have a copy of Kitty Wells's *Greatest Hits* – you had the band and Kitty sign it. Was it at a hall out in the Fraser Valley that my father may have been at?

Dear L. Hissey, I have the copy of Herbert Marcuse's *The Aesthetic Dimension* that you stamped your name in before Gail Jernberg or Ternberg, a subsequent owner, wrote her name below it.

Dear Deanna, I just picked up your copy of the Beatles's *Abbey Road* – I like how you wrote your name into the curve of the Apple Record label on both sides – green apple and cut apple.

Dear McEwan, I have your copy of *Close the 49th Parallel: The Americanization of Canada*, which has a Greg Curnoe painting as its cover, which is why I picked it up in Seattle.

I want to thank whoever got rid of the single of Bill Withers's "Use Me," it saves my life some days!

Dear Allyson, I got your copy of the catalogue for the *Some Detached Houses* show – was that the first exhibition that focused on housing and its coming disaster in Vancouver?

Dear K. Miller, the copy of Jonathan Raban's *Soft City* that I have comes with your name and phone number on the first page. I have not called to see if you still live there.

Dear Slocan Public Library, I have the red City Lights Books edition of William Carlos Williams's *Kora in Hell* that was either never returned or discarded: it makes me think of Fred Wah.

Dear Rochester Public Library, I treasure the copy of George Oppen's *Of Being Numerous* discarded from your Arnett Blvd. Branch: I carry it everywhere.

M.E. McGarry, did you also admire the beautiful minimal cover of Carl Rakosi's *Amulet* which I now have and as I do?

Dear Jerry Zaslove, I must have bought your copy of Georg Lukács, *Record of a Life* from a campus book sale – oh Jerry, you are so missed!

Dear K. Sekul, I have the copy of Denise Levertov's *A Door in the Hive* that you wrote in (in fountain pen) "July 1996 / U. of Washington Bookstore."

Dear Jane, I have your copy of Roberta Flack's *Quiet Fire* – OMG!

Dear Tanzschule Zemphera, I have Redbone's *The Witch of New Orleans* that you probably used to teach a particular dance style. Someone indicated "JIVE" in ballpoint beside the title track. Are you still on Gumpendorfer Strasse in Vienna?

Dear Chr., I have the copy of *Hard* by Gang of 4 you initialled – maybe you worked at a radio station, as it has a promotional-copy stamp on the back cover?

Dear T.J.A., I have your Cat Stevens *Catch Bull at Four* (lightly used, I note).

Dear Sheila, I have the hardcover of Charles Olson's *The Archaeologist of Morning* that Neil, robin, Liz, Chris, Rob, Eric, and Ian all signed with love to you: it is singularly touching.

Dear Lee, the copy of 1910 Fruitgum Co.'s *Indian Giver* that you wrote your name on in red has a cover still remarkable for its racism! Sadly, I too owned it in my youth.

Dear Werner Brosch, I have your perfect copy of Special AKA's *In the Studio* with its "smash-hit," "Nelson Mandela": but it's "Racist Friend" that resonates. Are you still on Blumengasse? – It's a fabulous street.

Hey, G. Spenser, I have your lovely copy of V. I. Lenin's *Imperialism: The Highest Stage of Capitalism*: as Russia invades Ukraine during this time of monopolies, it reads too present!

Dear S.D., I have your 45 of Slade's "Coz I Luv You": how did you dance to it in 1971?

Dear Jenny, I have the copy of *The Underachieving School* by John Holt you bought in January 1973. Did you also buy it in Woodstock, NY, where I bought it nearly fifty years later, waiting for Mark to pick me up to drive back to the city?

Dear Prabita, somewhere I picked up your copy of Fun Boy Three's debut album – it wears well.

Dear DAF, I have your twelve-inch single of Bananarama's "The Wild Life." Did you know Prabita, by chance?

Dear Mrs. Eva Kelamen, did you review Diane Wakoski's *The Motorcycle Betrayal Poems*? I now have your review copy.

Dear Louise, Ry Cooder's *Into the Purple Valley* has your name printed in your lovely script, upper right in the gatefold: Is your name there because you took it to listening parties?

Dear D.F. Cousineau, I just got your Erving Goffman *Encounters*: it has your name rubberstamped in beautiful sans-serif font and blue ink.

Dear Laberge, I have the vinyl of Bim's *Kid Full of Dreams* that you wrote your name on the back label of in 1975. I remember that year and perhaps we met?

Dear Carol H., your copy of Richard Hoggart's *The Uses of Literacy* has helped guide me for twenty-five years – I hope it did the same for you.

The discarded copy from SFU's library of Marcel Mauss's *The Gift* I take now as a gift with a responsibility to refute.

Dear Mary, your Chess Records copy of *Fathers and Sons*, the intergenerational blues project, is in my hands now.

Susan, in the copy of Gertrude Stein's *What Are Masterpieces?* that I have, Shel has written a note to you inside the cover: "The video meeting is in the cinema workshop."

Dear Bob, I picked up your copy of *The Politics of Despair* for the title and the cover design – inside it seems to be signed by the author, Hadley Cantril, "For Bob: pleasant memories of banghok – Hadley"– what's the story behind this?

My copy of Patti Smith's *Horses* is inscribed, on the cover just under the title and in a near-indecipherable German script, "I'm in Old Greenwich cannot sleep without my love."

ALL DAY LONG AND INTO THE NIGHT

Nighttime is the right
inversion
to relive the daytime

as a kind
of thought pandemic.

I can hardly stand my own lack
of efficiency tracked

as I enter
my work system

I berate myself:
Why can I not

do this better, more
effectively, really have

an impact like a meteorite
on a Monday

stamp out die-cast
decisions as a mighty

machine, stamping
through three shifts.

Working on the day shift
all night long!

Body across the clock
or was it the hour over the heart?

I will be away from email
I may be away from my desk

but my desk will be with me
wherever we go.

It is the desk
of the daughter
whose father did the books

for the egg company
we all know

or so she said as
we lifted it into the back
of the car.

It is her family
not mine.

Do you have any comments?
If so, we welcome

you, them. You
know.

What is the work, where
is the love? you might ask

Well, right back here
where we started from.

Why love, you might ask?

Ask away like a ship out on the sky!

Roberta, Donny – where
is the love?

Certainly
right there
with you

is where I want to be.

There is so little love
I can hardly rent a space

to breathe, or buy time
to tether to.

That is why (tell me
why!) I lean into

the camera for Zoom:

I make a connection.
A connection is made.

In my effective moments

which I feel
across the tides of time
we call the day

I hope you do too.

Can we call
it a day when it

won't go away
will not clock off?

"Negotiators are working
around the clock!"

This is my new Hello:
Are you
there now

is there
a now there

for us?

I APPROVE THE MINUTES

How do you work
when the world does not

or what you do
makes the world worse

or what you do makes you *feel* worse
and spreads across the days

as a catastrophe trophy and trumpet
of sector experts hired to help

with change-management heartbreak.
Hands up all those

who thought a job
was mutual! Uh huh, I thought so.

Red thread woven through work
forget it! I've internally

betrayed myself, a class
dream which was a *daydream*

to move from use
to life and back again.

My place of employment, my fall fashion
my esprit de corps announced:

We stand for Nothing.
Stand with us! Side by side

appropriately distanced and under contract
in empty spaces of solidarity.

It was not that I could not love
or care, but that I had not been trained

to evacuate that way, selectively
without setting a proper precedent.

The recommended training-module template
was not filled with the joy I expected

and the saddest cog was me –
I was the chair of the committee!

Not *comrade* or *sessel* or *silla*
or Enzo Mari's revolutionary Sedia 1!

Just a living job description, a narrative
of doing and knowing not

in that order, scribed
across a landscape of minds and visas

that did not make time
for daydreams from which

the future springs. It was
a silent spring, aside from wars

a semester in hell after a plague
of new policies and policing.

Through this we lost track
of who we were to be

a thousand wolves or the leader
of the pack – Johnny!

The bottom line or maybe
the high bar – hard to tell

outside of a pilot project –
was "do no harm," *do no harm*

was what to aim for, colleagues!
But that proved hard to meet

so we reported back that no
candidate was suitable. I had

stepped up and could not stoop.
If I am pledging my time

to cohesion then let time pledge
that it can bond other temporalities

and pay the mortgage on the present
for the education industry:

let it fling minds free, a centrifuge
and not come back hassling for tuition.

My apology is twofold: sorrow
and joy. It made me less human

to have to unfold the categories
of the human for others

to come into a software-compatible
rights-based form of recognition

like it was legit rather than
an unexploded shell from an earlier colony.

This was the tentative space set aside
to build new forms of human caring.

It might be *the Middle Ages*
of something, but it feels

like the end point of a time
negated, elated, and pleated

while lessons on unlearning *unlearning*
double down on a double

bind, the clear eyes and healthy hearts
of the "'outsiders' within"

working on rough translations
of the potential into the actual.

HOW TO KEEP BREATHING IN THE FUTURE

If it is to be mostly
optimistic in time
knowing a part of you
is already in the future
that started as a swerve
and ended with a small
solid encounter.

Each family teach one
until family amicably melts
like standard glaciers, replaced
with better basics or a communal
luxury funded by core and
care – it's my moss
that keeps me whole.

For each intensity felt
a deep dive not to
divide those working
on Mars and those owning
Mars or the right to Mars
or other planets of their youth
instead of extended extraction
– the great supply chain
of one man unto themselves
a monopoly
filling the skies.

It's too expensive to keep talking
each word a volume
of liquid gas through Ukraine
into a Europe with new
fences made from the old material –

wire, fear, cold
cobalt, the joined nations
held apart by water
please turn it
solid as the road
from recognition to negation.

It is not too early to lay
blame on the nineteen-nineties
because I surely feel that.

Another decade might
have been possible
for pushing your luck
or reading a book
and jumping
into an atmospheric
river.

"Own your own"
it was once said
by wise owners. Imagine
hearing that, your nose
pressed against the glass!

"A timeless attempt" to enter
the history of cinema
to start with workers leaving
not from a factory
but from their work-from-home day
going where?
Outta here!

Now that your
attention is the basis
of an economy

the work of "paying
attention" is not an idle
act: a moment is monetized
in some sweet surplus
action.

Your soul psychedelicized
through microdosing
until a high-risk present – your high-risk
present – is a shaky future
a dumpster fire
rolled at asylum seekers.

A microhome can be
the beginning
of a dream
that has already deferred
even before you
have woken up.

What could be better – how
about common wealth
or communal luxury
if you can imagine it.

It's so hard otherwise
because I have been trained
through threat, knowledge, and
practice to salvage pleasure
to enjoy strings and hop
beans and rice
breath and balance
a proprioceptive way
to live better longer
through the day the week the book.

Amazing to see
something made in a place
we know – and this is
at the heart of how
I can barely grasp
each day – than we are acclimatized
to cross-continent fires:
cause and effect
can be so startling
after the centuries.

I would like
it to be
brighter now
rather than later

TIME TO GET IT TOGETHER

When the itinerant farmworkers join up with the food rioters and the Saturday big-box shoppers, this whole industrial food complex is tumbling down!

When the students and the renter associations and the transit police and the bus drivers coalesce, it's more or less over for the venture capitalists and their adventure futures.

When the squatters and the dog walkers coordinate the brigades storming the empty buy-to-let owners' south-facing ecosensitive apartments, then the time is ripe and the seed is in the soil!

When the fireworkers and the fire ants unite with the unleashed hounds of postconceptual audience-participation artworks, there'll be the low spark of high-heeled lowballers – bosses under bosses will be undone!

When the Mennonites and the Hutterites unite and decolonize the acres that enticed for free, they'll cakewalk into town and tear it down, glass sheet by glass sheet, and autonomy will arise!

When the portfolio managers finally wake up and connect with North Macedonian hackers, a hack redistributes wealth faster than a plutocratic jet.

When the sharing economy shucks its huckster data-mining overlords and driverless cars are free-roaming pods for living, the monetizers will sink into the sea roiling with the heat of offshore computer banks.

When the universities are free and schools of mackerel swarm as high-speed flashes of silver coordinated by pods of syndicalist orcas, then we'll see who is jumping through hoops or eating their trainers.

When the touch-screen assemblers and the out-of-work brewery workers open the taps of euphoria and tap the apps of online banking diverting back to accounts of the low the money redistributed up, the lords of war and their campaign funders will wash away in a sea-curated foam.

When I can hear the children singing, "We are not the future in your image," the reproducers of the world Command-Option-Escape and a new world drawn from the old only much, much better will burst forth!

MY SHORT NOVEL

I was working in a gas station, a greenhouse, in delivery, in gardening, in editing, in teaching, in administration. The weather has a new name and it is no longer adorable. They gather to harass the healthcare workers for their freedom. The police wave their greetings. Defund and refund. Unravel it so DNA is living for others – can that be a future option? Searching for the comrade tree or more mutual aid with less family photos. Cut-and-paste was once the new editing where pure thought pulsed like a hard drive on the open range. I admit to wanting to write in paragraphs since some time in the 1980s. The sonic clash of architecture or a stack of notes built up by all the social forces (can we call them that?) into a soundscape (can we call it that?) that gathered us all here to reenact the past. They enter pretty predetermined. I saw minds. On a generation that squandered its future. Or the future for others?

How do you experience a day? My days are rather done, they take the shape of small temporary paper sculptures. Paper can help you cross a border, but not if you have made the paper. Or are made of paper. Sitting ships in the harbour rust with the sadness of continual time, time and time again, crossing the oceans, forlorn the cause of such grief. I try to talk you into the job, and then later you may be my boss. How did I get here? A local monument, a tribute to a gassy man was toppled today. Bring out the red paint! I will never buy the mayor's goat yogurt again. The money-laundering restaurant became popular and has stuck around. I worry about my optimism. Talking about your cataracts, not Atari, or Adirondack chairs, or breakaway Cascadia! On this humble corner, colonial beginnings have long been celebrated. Threw my microcredentials out the window, threw my diploma out there, too. A paragraph is sound. The new mayor regrets it was pulled down in an unsafe way. How can you legitimately develop a theme with an attention span like that? We fan out to other cities and later gather. I had months when a day, Tuesday, was fat and the cheque came.

I have repeatedly written that it was my stated ambition not to die of industrial cancer. That is the B-side of the present, a negative time that leads to the future. Are they blowing up their own pipelines to slow gas through their monopoly? The heads of town may move up to the aether or they can vaporize others. To clarify: how do you live when you do not have anywhere to live? This was a policy taken place to place. Universities call the police in a flash – then a flash from the police who love that it is 1970 again. The present is all I have to be present in, as the past never lived up to its promise. There in a brief leaf leapt life.

MY HARD EDGE PAINTINGS

after Pierre Coupey

My hard edge paintings
are a list
of demands
or plans where colour
rushes into
our kinetic future
on a hard-to-observe land
to so-called *light*
upon in the shadows
under the cover
of canvas, an advance
like walking out
into the city
and marvelling at the streets
those streets – the cut
edges of a hard
edge painting are there
for us all
a future today of
ocular optimistic
public and standing solid
with the invitation
where there was not
just one but many
not for the one
but for the many
times.

CONCEPTUALISM AFTER MINIMALISM

I had to think about it
New York School or Vancouver
School or Bohemian Forest
of critical regionalism landed
with a stoic granite sculpture

or a tree calling out
for use, standing straight
in a line with others
a line or a cut
on a canvas
that says there is nothing
to see as I
can't represent what is
exploding in front
of me.

Concepts after office minimalism
a clear calm way
to work when work
is the stretched canvas
frame of everything – again
when you asked
for a future, you
were given
an option
you could not befriend.

I loved it when
thought was productive
not extracted but pro-
tracted and off
the rails, off the

grid, a centrifuge
spinning peripheries.

I'm not denying I too
had to learn
how to think
the hardest things last
there was then
and did we together
burst to life and
life came to thought
as a camera.

TIME CATCHES

The architecture of this work is rooted in the temporal.
—FRANTZ FANON
   Black Skin, White Masks

That which is choking
you is also
choking me

but its tight mesh
is not yours

nor others
under a blight

I made it and

I will lose it last

that time

which you have

lived in

arrives

(already

"one cannot rise
and liberate oneself
in one area
and sink in an
other"

or swim

what can create
a condition
of sinking

an awful hour
back
in time

don't make it again
today

a dialectic
anticipating

that past
to come

where you have been
already

ready

"opposite occurs"

save us

"tight links"

t ght l nk s

subtracted to save

defund
———
defend

fend off

"the same time"

in the street

"impossible and shocking"

the same time

as a reminder

collective acts
_____

noncollective actors

time made

multiple

in the street
    square

decline inclusion

to be included

that's an implied time

(imposed)

and who would want to join
in that clock

with its shock of the utter
lack of life

the time

we stop stifling you

opens another time

first for us

as you are ahead

already there

a day a form
of freedom

cities edged

in flames
not a "fire season"

shared across Europe / Americas
cutting through the middle

five hundred degree wind
through a boreal forest

but cops in cars
and youth
who want
to not be shot

but to breathe

no "new fires"

a low day
a day
behind
a measure

a pressure
in cities

        so close in place

a closed solace

            on a colonial clock

what is near

lightning / strike
not once but

clash

on the ground:

port	university
forest	land
city	square
property	knowledge
tight	time

flash, he said

not the usual

wet coastal ground

I hope by analyzing it to destroy it.
—**FRANTZ FANON**
　Black Skin, White Masks

LATE FASCISM, EARLY AFTERNOON

When the Vienna police

opened
and allowed

the column of young men

I thought
they were holding back

to walk in

a line, chanting
clear strong
borders and purity

a proud line
across the public *denkmal*

time suddenly aligned
not in synch

not happening again
but still

(The US Embassy in Austria issues a "Demonstration Alert" of "self-described 'Antifa' demonstrators" against a fascist "Identitarian" rally)

A SAD GAIN

a sad gain a hard
grain a cold
card a core worry
a sour hour a
sincere fold a cut
curfew a folded few
a sturdy day a
struck neck
a dropped knee a cut
blue a capped
camp a angled
tent a city shelter
a common monologue
a civic crisis a city
yet a coveted
street a factory
door a ancient
glass a short
taunt a long truant
a shared red
a military
presence a doubted
cloud a wrong
head a hard
rung a tungsten
hiring a appropriate end
a down amount a pollen
burst a burned
window a sad self a
cared self a violent
space a curved attempt
a sharp explain a sudden
room a calculated

cut a void space a
boiled wool a wooden
response a poised
answer a frightening
toll a transient
toil a salty
entry a immediate
gain a action
item a mediated
aim a monday name
a sunday frame a full
stop a fecund
second a heard third a thwarted
first a onus
proposal a honest nest
a dropped forge a fallen
dollar a lapsed
salmon a caught
breath a casual
cough a rough nest
a composed calm a worried
wood a diligent
city a struck
street a speculated
space a blind bid
a held house a distanced
cedar a red air a dear
reader a darkened garden a
green recovery a hour cowered
a time spent a day covered
a composed moment a may
day a workers kern
a rented shed a decimated
figure a spread excel a
fought right a shared time
a laboured space a imagined

tool a aluminum
toil a oil fugitive
a twisted wish a wealth
gain a shunned union
a ammunition
shortage a urgent
ask a due diligence
a obliterated
city a spatial
gain a hopeful
ovoid a turned
valve a other
value

THE MOST BEAUTIFUL THING

after Scritti Politti

The most beautiful thing
may be this bend of beech
that makes the back
of this chair

the most beautiful thing
may be the time
taken to shape
that elegant function

or the most beautiful thing
may have been the tree
cultivated to be changed
nature from first to second

or the most beautiful thing
might be the work
of the person who shaped
that one bend in the metal

made from iron ore
dug shipped processed rolled
into a tube designed now
an aesthetic angle

or the most beautiful thing
may be that song
conceived sung and heard
to be shared a beautiful thing

for *the value of defiance*
in a turn of a year
when *sweetest* might
have been imagined otherwise

or the most beautiful thing
may be the space you make
it as you imagine it
conceived built inhabited altered

by an encounter that swerves
to what is possible
an act an action
an unscripted learning

URBAN TREES

are all trees urban now?

fifty years less than half
white paper birch what will
now bring you down old
high water wildfires jumping lake
narrows or campers a new

slice of mountain sliding down
wind emergent extremes truss trees
to cities urban ongoing displaced
causes one white birch beside
cedar wild rose lake planet

willow trees for lost lagoon

willow weep on a lost
lagoon lost from the tide's
sweep up now a park
value-added to the enclosed welcome
of a statue's open arms

why this string of willows
yellow in spring a wet
soil lake edge decision planted
here now cracking limbs wet
dry excess rhythm historic drought

managed trunks as urban data
crews haul out chipper truck
what use here now trees
an idea of image city
park with heavy willows welcome

address to the city

i see what you have
done – trees cut and chipped
the story of their health
merely maintenance and city safety
move from common to commodity

a city's idea of trees
manager of low-value species culling
susceptible species planning species richness
speculating high-value species street trees
windthrow detritus disease and risk

no cover for people pushed
into the park ground rent
abstracts ground pulls trees into
this clash control green space
a cleanup against botanical justice

can we call a city
cruel a revanchist urban jurisdiction
an act managing imagined nature
an uneven economy of green
don't implicate trees in that

a city's idea of itself (political economy of trees)

kwanzan flowering cherry pissard plum
norway maple western red cedar
crimean linden red maple pyramidal
european hornbeam night purple leaf
plum kobus magnolia european beech

bowhall red maple douglas fir
katsura tree common horsechestnut akebono
flowering cherry hedge maple american
elm armstrong red apple pin
oak red oak sycamore maple

columnar norway maple european hornbeam
pacific sunset maple london plane
tree japanese flowering crabapple japanese
flowering cherry japanese snowbell autumn
applause ash redbud crabapple *order*

address to a country tree

elegant fallen birch proprioceptive slumber
to lumber cut contour of
fire road fir cedar alder
quartz crushed underbrush a quick
catastrophic loop against spark jump

trees and shelter

out of necessity a canopy
in birch hazelnut cedar elder
a blind for stretched tarp
detritus tin and plastic sheets
precarious house hidden in trees

on a highway meridian strip
space spun past city periphery
farmland roads suburb ovals and
grid strata of how land
is used in this logic

past municipal cruelty and between
two lanes a discreet space
outside of property and into
the trees as support cover
before winter bare trees life

"the battle over Sheffield's street trees"

17,500 street trees removal and
replacement pushed through private contract
for public trees a battle
of people guardians for legal
shadow trees all over (again)

there are no such things
as trees echo past cuts
social and natural tally replayed
split not how people live
trees and root of austerity

future trees

arizona cypress hackberry lampion ginkgo
bilboa japanese raisin bee-bee tree
move as chosen future trees
for an "assisted migration" south
to north to cultivate "future-proof

livable city" where the trees
suit future weather the language
of human migration inverted onto
seeds trees growth species *exotics*
the fate of existing trees

workers' cuffs

seed pod pant cuff traveller
workers of the earth carry
future trees cuffed up in
rolled pant caught in boot
tread trees into the city

a continuous urban ground remake
paths of work walk transport
shipping container global cuff unfolded
brings trees along routes paths
migration of labour bodies seeds

brownfield pussy willows

look a basket of light
on an angled season out
of natural time grey fuzzed
bud a chime of climate
this february marking a making

record climbs a warning graph
a consecutive arc on train
tracks weeds where species wander
in cracks asphalt brick and
time gets hotter earlier now

bombing soil

the soil of bombed cities
so altered cannot grow so-called
indigenous trees in dirt made
by war mingled with pulverized
buildings homes a devastated dirt

calcium lime ash carbon bones
burnt and turned over emerges
first *disaster flora* as new
urban cover unpredictable saplings follow
burnt trunks shrapnel bark trees

less natural and stressed in
wounded cities the soil-forming event
of bombs and species choice
a tree knows the soil
but not that it's bombed

bombing trees

trees of Kyiv trees of
Gaza City trees of Beirut
trees of Borodianka trees of
Aden trees of Kharkiv trees
of Marib trees of Al Hudaydah

trees of the "War of
the Cities" trees of Derna
trees of Smara trees of
Aleppo trees of Damascus trees
of Halabja trees of Djibo

trees of Rafah trees of
Ayta al-Sha'b trees of Vovchansk trees
of Avdiivka trees of the
West Bank trees of Sanaa
trees of Marawi trees of

neurological canopy

the aging city and synapses
need over 20% tree canopy
to drop odds of dementia
green *allée* neurology of linden
better choose your neighbourhood carefully

ungovernable trees

where and how trees grow
is governed through bodily sway
neglect or care as other
bodies a shared social forest
deemed city or private property

a governed tree can surprise
rise and spread against rule
break property cracks and roots
an ecology under an economy
an unruly process sprouts encounters

urban trees do not comply
easily refuse to be governed
like *that* refuse the city
order refuse to be displaced
trees grow unruly use instead

trees and people porous bodies
not commodities even when they
give shelter give health redefine
water hold soil are homes
trees work against being governed

trees in "The Indian Act, 1876"

"The term 'reserve' means any
tract or tracts of land
set apart by treaty or
otherwise for the use or
benefit of or granted to

a particular band of ~~Indians~~,
of which the legal title
is in the Crown but
which is unsurrendered, and includes
all the trees, wood, timber,

soil, stone, minerals, metals or
other valuables thereon or therein
... in such a manner as
the Governor in Council may
direct." trees grow other crowns

"Should Trees Have Standing?"

making *persons* of trees bends
from rightless thing in nature
to jural entity but blocks
another order not defined by
that trick of singular recognition

"common law makes things rightless"
and to gain rights joins
the very category you are
outside of enter an episteme
built upon a solid outside

for humans who hold rights
at the time a space
that alters over time to
take in trusts corporations inanimate
rightsholders and exclude other humans

from thing to human and
back again incorporated nature property
trees do you want to
have such a standing or
stand outside of such thought

searching for the comrade tree

why mother family form for
trees *ursprung* leave them their
own rhizomic matters not familial
a division of labour social
mutual aid grounded in another

something entirely else not us
our forms pressed whole on
another after historic failure crush
as one comrade to another
nods "don't cut me down"

tree cities of the world

spectre of total area coverage
city trees rise unite and
take over with better urban
arbour labour take a day
a month trees have time

A tree in Vienna, Austria, during a pro-democracy / antifascist march, October 2, 2024.
Photo: Jeff Derksen

Urban tree Cairo
PHOTO: Jeff Derksen

NOTES ON SOURCES, REFERENCES, AND INSPIRATIONS

"Forty Days and Eight Hundred Nights" refers to Muddy Waters's classic 1956 version of "Forty Days and Forty Nights" (written by Bernard Roth).

"Living Through Aluminum" is in dialogue, or in solidarity, with Pat Lowther's poem "Chacabuco, the pit" from *A Stone Diary* (posthumously published in 1977 by Oxford University Press). I was first introduced to Lowther's work by the poet and teacher Leona Gom.

The poem also contains a productive misreading of the lines "As the dead prey upon us, / they are the dead in ourselves" from Charles Olson's "As the Dead Prey Upon Us." A July 7, 2015, *CBC News* article, "Kitimat Rio Tinto Aluminum Smelter Re-opens" is also quoted.

The literal sources of the books and records that form "More Poems About Books and Records" are the various bookstores, record shops, thrift stores, street markets, *Flohmärkt*, charity shops, and the stoops, steps, and corners where people recirculate music and words. And the great pleasures of circulation, reading, and listening.

"I Approve the Minutes" draws inspiration and life from the late radical educator Mike Neary's *Student as Producer: How Do Revolutionary Teachers Teach?* (Zer0 Books, 2020) and Amy De'Ath's *Not a Force of Nature* (Futurepoem, 2024).

"Time Catches" evolved from the anticolonial possibilities of time in Frantz Fanon's work, particularly *A Dying Colonialism* (Grove Press, 1965), *Black Skin, White Masks* (Grove Press, 1967), and *The Wretched of the Earth* (Présence Africaine, 1963). I also refer to Asef Bayat's concept of "collective acts" and "noncollective actors" from his *Life as Politics: How Ordinary People Change the Middle East* (Stanford University Press, second edition, 2013) and in conversations with him at Die neue Gesellschaft für bildende Kunst (nGbK) events in Berlin (thanks to Jochen Becker). I have written about temporality and colonialism in other formats, including "Canadian Literature and the Temporality of Dying Colonialism," *University of Toronto Quarterly* 89, no. 1 (2020).

"Late Fascism, Early Afternoon" refers to Alberto Toscano, *Late Fascism: Race, Capitalism, and the Politics of Crisis* (Verso, 2023).

"The Most Beautiful Thing" is in dialogue with the Scritti Politti song "The 'Sweetest Girl'" (written by Green Gartside) from the 1982 album *Songs to Remember*. I think I first heard the song via one of Peter Culley's now-legendary mix-tape gifts.

As a research poem, "Urban Trees" draws broadly on work in urban geography, urban botany, climate change, and the work of nonprofit and community organizations that promote and defend urban forests and street trees. "Should Trees Have Standing?" refers to Christopher D. Stone, "Should Trees Have Standing – Toward Legal Rights for Natural Objects," *Southern California Law Review* 45 (1972): 450–501. "bombing soil" is informed by Seth Denizen, "The flora of bombed areas (an allegorical key)" and Sonia Dümpelmann, "Seeing, Surveying, and Sorting Urban Trees: the 1970s Street Tree Project in Dresden," both in *The Botanical City*, eds. Matthew Gandy and Sandra Jasper (jovis, 2020). My thinking on the effects of war on street trees is also informed by Judith Stilgenbauer and Joe R. McBride, "Reconstruction of Urban Forests in Hamburg and Dresden After World War II," *Landscape Journal* 29, no. 2 (2010): 144–160. Some of my thoughts on spatial and botanical justice were informed by Nikolas C. Heynen, "The Scalar Production of Injustice within the Urban Forest," *Antipode* 35, no. 5 (2003): 980–998.

The poem also benefited from specific site visits to Dresden (Germany), Berlin (Germany), Vienna (Austria), Bern (Switzerland), Vancouver and the Nahatlatch Valley.

"Urban Trees" is informed poetically by Louis Zukosfky's *80 Flowers* and his unfinished project *GAMUT: 90 Trees*. Fred Wah's *Tree* (1972, also in *Scree* [Talonbooks, 2015]) is a fundamental influence, and I quote the poem "Don't Cut Me Down" in "searching for the comrade tree."

Urban tree Cairo
PHOTO: Sabine Bitter

ACKNOWLEDGMENTS

Some of these poems have appeared in earlier versions in *Tripwire*, *The Capilano Review*, *Canada and Beyond* (translated into Castellano by Isaac Xubín), the Poetry Foundation website, and *Some*. Thanks to Brandon Brown for his commentary on "In Memory of My Heavy Metal Years" in his blog on the Poetry Foundation website.

My gratitude to Louis Cabri for his careful reading and edits of this collection of poems and for our friendship. Our conversations in Vancouver over 2023 shaped these works into a book (even when I didn't see it). I'd also like to thank Jordan Scott for key conversations and encouragement, which happily happened over beers in several cities.

Thank you to Catriona Strang, ryan fitzpatrick, Leslie Smith, and everyone else at Talonbooks for your support and patience as this went from manuscript to book. Catriona's comments and edits very beautifully tailored the final version. Thanks as well to Michael Nardone for conversations about the possibility of poetry books.

Thanks to Pierre Coupey for permission to use a painting from his "Terminal Series" (1968–1969) for the cover.

I had the opportunity to try out versions of these poems at readings at People's Co-op Books, Vancouver, Red May, Seattle, Librairie Drawn & Quarterly, Montréal, and other venues and moments. Thank you to the organizers.

This book was written over the fragmentation of years, but it is grounded in the cities and territories that I was fortunate to be hosted or live in: Vancouver (so-called, on the unceded Territory of the xʷməθkʷəy̓əm, Sḵwx̱wú7mesh, and səlilwətaɬ); the Nahatlatch Valley, BC (Nlaka'pamux Nation Territory); Aigen, Upper Austria; and Vienna.

Urban tree Vancouver
PHOTO: Jeff Derksen

THANK YOU

Gail Scott, Dorothy Trujillo Lusk, Kevin Davies, Kathy Slade, Kay Higgins, Clint Burnham, Steve Collis, Cecily Nicholson, Phinder Dulai, Mercedes Eng, David Buuck, Kelly Wood, Fred Wah, Pauline Butling, Am Johal, Althea Thauberger, Elspeth Pratt, Javier Campos, Johanne Sloan, Amy De'Ath, Danielle LaFrance, Mark Nowak, Lisa Arrastia, Rodrigo Toscano, Rita Wong, Henry Hills, Rob Manery, Michael Barnholden, Nicole Markotić, A Jamali Rad, Lina Leonore Morawetz, Nils Jensen, Richard Cavell, Colin Browne, Marian Penner Bancroft, Stefan Römer, Scott Inniss, Jo Giardini, Robert Yerachmiel Sniderman, Nero Gogalic, Fintan Calpin, Katie McNaughton, Cole Mash, Craig Derksen, Lynn Bueckert, Helmut Weber and the Kohlenrutsche Gemeinschahft Wien, Café Else (Vienna), Freibad Aigen-Schlägl, Pale Fire afterhours (Vancouver), Laguna Vista Apartments (Vancouver).

Dorothy Cucw-la7 Christian and the Indigenous Working Group at Simon Fraser University for the teachings and the joking!

And to Sabine Bitter – art into life, life into art every day.

Urban tree Vienna
PHOTO: Sabine Bitter

JEFF DERKSEN is a poet, critic, and professor who lives in Vancouver (unceded xʷməθkʷəy̓əm, Sk̲wx̲wú7mesh, and səlilwətaɬ territories) and Vienna (Austria). His poetry books include *The Vestiges*, *Transnational Muscle Cars*, and *Down Time* (Winner of the Dorothy Livesay Poetry Prize). His critical books include *After Euphoria*, *Annihilated Time: Poetry and Other Politics*, and the folio *How High is the City, How Deep is Our Love*. He works on artistic research projects with the collective Urban Subjects: their books include *The Militant Image Reader*, *Momentarily: Learning from Mega Events*, and *Autogestion: Henri Lefebvre in New Belgrade*. As curators, they brought *The Vienna Model: Housing for the 21st Century* to the Museum of Vancouver and curated the exhibition *If Time Is Still Alive* at Camera Austria. He was a founding member of both the Kootenay School of Writing and Artspeak Gallery. Derksen works at Simon Fraser University and is a Fulbright Fellow and former research fellow at the Centre for Place, Culture, and Politics at The Graduate Center, CUNY.